D0787603

VA 306.1
Acker, Kerry.
Everything you need to know
about the Goth scene
New York : Rosen Pub. Group
2000.

Discarded by
Santa Maria Library

02   09   10   I1109
I   I   7| 11

Everything
You Need to
Know About

The
Goth
Scene

Goths often sport unusual hair, makeup, and clothing, and are fascinated with mysterious and frightening things.

Everything You Need to Know About

The Goth Scene

Kerry Acker

The Rosen Publishing Group, Inc.
New York

For my parents

Published in 2000 by The Rosen Publishing Group, Inc.
29 East 21st Street, New York, NY 10010

Copyright © 2000 by The Rosen Publishing Group, Inc.

First Edition

All rights reserved. No part of this book may be reproduced in any form without permission in writing from the publisher, except by a reviewer.

Library of Congress Cataloging-in-Publication Data

Acker, Kerry
   Everything you need to know about the Goth scene / by Kerry Acker.—1st ed.
      p.   cm. —(The need to know library)
Includes bibliographical references and index.
   ISBN 0-8239-3223-0 (library binding)
   1. Goth culture (Subculture) [1. Goth culture (Subculture)] I. Title.
II. Series.
   HQ796 .A2454 2000
   306'.1—dc21
                              00-008727

Manufactured in the United States of America

Contents

Introduction

*O*n April 20, 1999, at Columbine High School in Littleton, Colorado, two students opened fire on their schoolmates, killing thirteen people and wounding many others before finally shooting themselves, thereby ending their own lives as well. It was a bloody, terrible tragedy, which has left a permanent scar on the school, the community, and the entire country.

Dylan Klebold and Eric Harris, the two murderers, often wore black clothes and trench coats. Their style and clothing suggested that they were perhaps involved with the Goth scene. After the murders, many people—influenced by journalists, reporters, and other members of the media—started to look more closely at the Goth, *or Gothic, culture. Filled with anger and confused as to who was to blame for this horrible massacre, many people began to believe the Goth scene, and the beliefs and ideas associated with it, was somehow responsible for the shootings.*

People feared that all Goths were as troubled and violent as Klebold and Harris, and that all Goths were gun-loving and dangerous. Many people focused on the killers' apparent link to the Goth scene instead of looking at such other factors as Klebold's and Harris's troubled psychological histories or their access to weapons. The truth is, there are many different kinds of people in the Goth scene. And most of them are non-violent, quiet, and peaceful. As Ryan Mrazik, a twenty-seven-year-old Goth from Wisconsin, said in U.S. News & World Report, *"The overwhelming majority of Goths are quiet and introspective, much preferring a good horror novel to a bare-knuckle fight."*

The Goth scene is filled with people that look and dress very differently from most of the rest of society. Many Goths dress all in black, have uncommon hairstyles, and often wear black lipstick, nail polish, and makeup that makes them appear pale and ghostlike. And because they look different, many people are prejudiced against them. People judge Goths based on their clothing tastes and their appearance, instead of getting to know them by talking with them, hearing their ideas, and trying to find things in common with them. Because most people in the mainstream don't understand the typical Goth look, lifestyle, and philosophy, they are often leery of Goths. Goths became scapegoats after the Columbine murders. People—adults and students alike—started to blame the Goth scene without really understanding what it is. Kids were sent home from school for dressing "strangely" and authorities actually set up phone hotlines so students could turn in "odd" or "weird" peers. Many Goths felt this scapegoating and prejudice was unfair.

What does it mean to be Goth? People in the Goth scene come from a variety of different backgrounds and have different tastes, ideas, religions, and opinions. But there are some common traits, styles, and beliefs that many Goths share. They are often highly imaginative people, and being Goth provides a mode of self-expression and a forum for their creativity. Many Goths are drawn to a certain type of music, have a fascination with mysterious and frightening things, and are attracted to the darker aspects of life. The Goth scene provides them with a community of similar-minded people, where they can share their thoughts and ideas, listen to similar types of music, and feel a sense of belonging.

Many people might just dress Goth and go to Goth nightclubs, but not consider themselves Goth. Others might adopt aspects of the Goth style and way of life. Still others might listen to Goth music but not subscribe to the Goth philosophy. And some people make it their life.

After the murders at Columbine, the media began focusing on the parts of the Goth scene that are very extreme, such as satanism and vampirism. Although there are small groups of people in the Goth scene that do practice vampirism or satanism, most people in the Goth scene do not adhere to these belief systems. It is the media's negative portrayal that has caused much misunderstanding about what it means to be in the Goth scene.

This book will help you understand what Goth is and that it means different things to different people.

Chapter One

The Origins of Goth

The terms "Goth" and "Gothic" have been used throughout history to identify different peoples, movements, and styles. Understanding the history of Goth will help you understand how the modern Gothic style, sensibility and attitude developed.

The Original Goths

The original Goths were a tribe of Germanic peoples that probably originated in southern Scandinavia. The Goths invaded the Roman Empire in the early centuries of the Christian era. They divided into two separate groups in the late 200s and early 300s: the Visigoths (who became the first independent barbaric nation in the Roman Empire in 382) and the Ostrogoths (who were conquered by the Huns in the 370s). Both the

The original Goths were a Germanic tribe that invaded the Roman Empire in the early Christian era.

Visigoths and the Ostrogoths were influential in the ultimate collapse of the western Roman Empire. Because of this history of pillaging and looting, the term "Gothic" came to be associated with being barbaric (savagely cruel, or lacking civility and taste).

Gothic Art and Architecture

During the Renaissance—a period of great revival of art and learning that flourished in Europe during the fourteenth through sixteenth centuries—Italian scholars believed the classical arts had been altered and corrupted by the savage Goths. Their general feeling was that the architecture and art of the period, like the Goths themselves, were barbaric and unrefined. Although most people today consider Gothic art and architecture to be beautiful, passionate, and inspiring, Renaissance thinkers thought it was unsophisticated.

Gothic art and architecture reflected the intense mysticism of the Middle Ages (500–1500 AD), an era in which the Christian church held tremendous influence. The type of building most typical of Gothic architecture is the cathedral. Architects incorporated stained glass and stone gargoyles (grotesque human or animal figures) with large open interior spaces, pointed arches, and enormous columns. They made their buildings very tall to express religious glorification and importance. The first Gothic buildings appeared in France in the 1100s, and by the 1200s, Gothic architecture had spread to other parts of Europe. Some famous Gothic churches include Chartres and Notre Dame in France, Cologne Cathedral in Germany, and Westminster Abbey in England.

Gothic Literature

Gothic literary style developed in late eighteenth- and early nineteenth-century England. Gothic novels and stories teem with images of dimly lit castles, eerie lights, and trapdoors. Gothic authors explored, and even celebrated, the grotesque and the supernatural (spirits, ghosts, and events that aren't from the physical world). Their work was filled with horror and mystery. Gothic

Stone gargoyles were a common element of medieval Gothic architecture.

literature usually evokes a desolate landscape that is secluded and decaying. Part of the Romantic movement, Gothic literature blossomed during this period primarily as a rebellion against the sunny optimism that characterized the Enlightenment. The Gothic authors reminded readers that irrational impulses, fear, and darkness are inherent aspects of human nature.

The first Gothic novel that appeared in England was *The Castle of Otranto* (1764) which is a short novel by Horace Walpole set against a backdrop of dark forests, ruins, and gloomy landscapes. Other famous European Gothic novels include Ann Radcliffe's *Mysteries of Udolpho* (1794) and *Romance of the Forest* (1791), and Mary Wollstonecraft Shelley's *Frankenstein* (1818), a classic much loved by contemporary Goths (the book is also considered the first science fiction novel). The Marquis de Sade is another important Gothic figure, known for drawing attention to mankind's darkest traits and ugliest passions in such works as *Justine* (1791) and *Crimes of Love* (1800).

Most scholars consider Gothic literature to include only those works from the late eighteenth and early nineteenth centuries. For many other readers, Gothic literature refers to any work of fiction that idealizes or romanticizes the medieval period, overtly refers to the supernatural, draws on suspense and mystery, emphasizes morbid imagery, or creates a dark and gloomy atmosphere. This loose definition of Gothic literature includes the works of writers such as Bram Stoker and Charlotte Brontë and American authors Edgar Allen Poe, Flannery O'Connor, and Anne Rice. Poppy Z. Brite, Storm Constantine, and H. P. Lovecraft are also part of this genre. (See chapter 5.)

Contemporary Goth

Many people believe that the modern Gothic culture—the Goth movement, people, and lifestyles that are explored in this book—grew out of a musical style and sensibility that emerged from the punk scene, which started in England in the late 1970s. (There are other Goths, however, who insist that the modern Gothic culture was around long before the music.) Although it is unclear who first labeled this brand of music as Goth, most fans and critics trace the beginnings of the musical genre to the release of the band Bauhaus's "Bela Lugosi's Dead" in 1979. (See chapter 5.)

The Music

Goth used to be classified as a subdivision of punk rock, a musical style that is usually blatantly offensive, aggressively expresses anger at the state of society, and challenges the status quo. But as the punk scene slowly fizzled out, the Goth movement grew. Such bands as Bauhaus, Siouxsie and the Banshees, The Cure, and the Sisters of Mercy, created moodier, more introspective music that was less overtly rebellious than that of the punk bands. Whereas punk musicians and performers expressed their anger outwardly, the Goths were focused inward.

The band Bauhaus (named after the early twentieth century German architecture and design school founded by Walter Gropius), often considered the "Grandfathers of Goth," set the standard for other Goth rock bands with their imaginative live performances. Their intensely dark theatrics, costumes and makeup, and powerful imagery contributed to the Goth aesthetic, or idea of beauty. Siouxsie and the Banshees and the Sisters of Mercy reinforced this aesthetic by wearing primarily black clothing, dying their hair black, and applying pale makeup.

Many music journalists labeled these groups Goth, although many of the bands didn't consider themselves as such. Some journalists took to calling any bands that dressed all in black and wore pale make-up Goth, although their music was often quite different from that of Bauhaus or Siouxsie and the Banshees.

The Culture

The Goth music scene became the basis for a distinct view of the world and how to live in it. People of different backgrounds were drawn to this music and the lifestyle with which it became associated. An entire subculture slowly took shape. Like Siouxsie Sioux of Siouxsie and the Banshees and The Cure's Robert Smith, legions of Goths (male and female) lightened their skin, applied black lipstick, and donned black clothing. Those who took to the scene tended to share the belief that society had lost sight of what was important in life and had become too concerned with money. Goths wanted to experience emotions, good and bad, because they are an essential part of being human. Goths also thought that there was a lot of hatred and violence in the world, and that most people were ignoring it, walking around pretending they were happy. Goths also established a different idea of beauty—a new aesthetic. The contemporary Goth scene was born.

Although many Goth bands split up or changed their musical style, the Goth scene (although smaller)

Siouxsie and the Banshees were among the first bands to be identified as Goth.

continued. In the 1990s the scene was injected with new life. Bands sprang up that labeled themselves Goth (becoming the first to deliberately do so). Some of these bands were London After Midnight and Rosetta Stone. In the mid-1990s, industrial music and harder bands, such as Nine Inch Nails, Rammstein, and KMFDM, emerged. Although most Goths from the original scene reject this newer and harder, more technologically progressive music, a new younger generation of Goths embrace it.

In the late 1990s and in 2000, the Goth scene has grown substantially, yet it has divided and expanded into many different smaller branches, belief systems, and minicultures, increasingly distorting and re-creating the definition of what it means to be "Goth." Some that view themselves as Goth might not be considered true "Goths" by others. Some Goths will be a part of the scene for their entire life; others will just dabble in the scene for a brief while. For some, being Goth is a way of life, a lifestyle choice; for others, it is merely a style choice.

Finally, the media has contributed to a distorted popular view of Goths. Magazines, movies, television shows, and newspapers have created a Goth stereotype. Like all stereotypes, the Goth stereotype is over-simplified, and often misleading.

Chapter Two

Gothic Philosophy

The Goth scene encompasses a broad range of people. There is much disagreement in the Goth community as to what Goth is, so bear in mind that in this book we are merely going to explore the most basic ideas of Gothic philosophy and style. Although Goths include people of different politics, ages, races, religions, backgrounds, and careers, Goths do generally share some common lifestyle choices.

Goths often explore and express the deepest, darkest parts of themselves and of human nature. Goths believe that the dark parts of the soul are just as important as the brighter parts. They recognize that sorrow, sadness, fear, and even pain are essential parts of the human condition. They focus on those dark parts because they see beauty in them. To the Goth, dark does not mean evil. They think that these blacker elements are essential to a full life and are, therefore, beautiful. This emphasis on suffering, sorrow, fear, and death attracts many Goths to the night, spooky things, cemeteries, vampires, and horror in general. And witches, spirits, werewolves, ghosts, and the paranormal intrigue many Goths.

Goths accept different political leanings, different religious beliefs, different sexual preferences, and many different lifestyles that are often not accepted by mainstream culture. Many reporters have mistakenly associated Goth with white supremacy and extreme violence. Most Goths, however, are pacifists (against violence) and very tolerant. And most won't tolerate racism, sexism, or other types of discrimination.

Goths tend to be creative, imaginative, emotional, and sensual. They are often intense, dramatic, and take self-expression very seriously. To Goths, feeling the whole range of emotions means being alive. Fashion, poetry, art, music, and other creative outlets allow them to express themselves.

Being a Goth is one way to experience the world without adhering to or being pacified by mainstream rules.

Who Are Goths?

As stated above, followers of the Goth aesthetic include people of different ages, sensibilities, religions, politics, and careers. Some Goths go to school, are married, have children, or have careers—even corporate ones. Goths are a group of people with broad interests, such as history, literature, music, mythology, and fashion.

Some people become involved in the Goth scene because they identify with the philosophy of those involved in the scene and it gives them an arena in which to express those feelings freely. Many Goths are drawn to the scene because they have at some point felt different or alienated from others, or were labeled by others as different or weird. The Goth scene provides them with a sense of belonging. Goths might also have different sexual leanings, seem overly imaginative, or too creative or artistic for the mainstream. Goths tend to identify with outcasts and underdogs, people that feel alienated from others and from society as a whole.

Not all Goths listen to the same music, wear all black, or hang out looking gloomy. Mainstream culture has even embraced aspects of Goth as evidenced in the popularity of TV shows such as *Buffy the Vampire Slayer, The X-Files,* and *Charmed,* and the novels of Anne Rice. Many people dress Goth or are interested in aspects of the culture but don't necessarily live the Gothic philosophy.

Finally, some people (such as the Columbine killers, Klebold and Harris) adopt the Goth appearance and persona simply for the purpose of shocking people.

The recent success of TV shows like *Buffy the Vampire Slayer* is an indication that Gothic themes have become trendy.

Attraction to Darkness

As stated above, one of the most important parts of the Gothic aesthetic is the attraction to darkness (literal and symbolic darkness). Goths believe that darkness is just as powerful and important as light. Goths are drawn to things that are mysterious and otherworldly. (Remember, darkness does not mean evil. It can refer to things such as moonlit nights, cobwebs, haunted houses, graveyards, and candle-lit rooms.) What many Goths find beautiful might be considered ugly, frightening, or gross to others. Goths tend to be extreme with their tastes.

Goths find sadness, despair, and pain fascinating. These topics are often avoided and ignored by most of our culture—including parents and peers. Goths are not afraid of these feelings, as their goal is to experience the full range of life's emotions. Goths are constantly trying to get in touch with their emotions. To Goths, feeling is the best way to truly experience being alive. Goths do find death interesting, because they recognize it as a part of the life cycle. But that does not mean that Goths are obsessed with death or that they advocate hurting or killing others. Again, Goths believe that we must understand death to fully understand and appreciate life.

Goths and Depression

Much of our culture looks down on depression, viewing it as something that is not normal or that should be avoided or shunned. But depression is nothing to be ashamed of. It affects many people at different points in their lives. Many teens are prone to depression, as adolescence is an extremely difficult time. Adolescents experience peer pressure, pressure from their family, and pressure from society. It is a time of great emotional turmoil and heightened sensitivity.

Many Goths spend a lot of time thinking. They tend to be in touch with their emotions and have little problem showing their sadness or angst to the world. A lot of teens, and people in general, try to hide their feelings of inadequacy or sadness. Goths probably don't feel any sadder than others, but they usually don't try to hide it like most people do. In fact, some Goths even flaunt it as part of their identity or explore those feelings more deeply to get a full understanding of that emotional state.

Some Goths do have sullen tendencies. Because Goths are usually very sensitive and compassionate people, they might be extra sensitive to the pain of others and the pain of the world in general. But many Goths do have a sense of humor. This humor is typically very morbid, and it verges on self-parody. In other words, many Goths don't take themselves too seriously.

Depression, however, should not to be taken lightly. If anyone you know exhibits any of the following, they might be suffering from a depressive disorder:

- Profound loss of energy
- Change in sleeping habits, difficulty getting up for school
- Change in eating habits
- Lack of motivation
- Drop in grades
- Alcohol or drug abuse

If anyone you know exhibits these tendencies, let them know that it's okay to feel sad, but encourage them to talk to a teacher, a friend, a parent, or a counselor.

Goths and Death

Many people believe that Goths think too much about death. As mentioned before, many Goths think about death in order to understand and not be afraid of it. Many Goths think about death because they are interested in immortality—thus explaining their interest in entities like Dracula. Some Goths are simply fascinated by the mystery of death and all of the intriguing things that surround it—coffins, graveyards, ghosts, and other morbid subjects. Most of us are intrigued by death, we usually just aren't as open about it. Most Goths do not believe in violence and do not advocate hurting or killing others.

Many Goths are fascinated with the mystery of death and the occult.

Of course, there are some people who are troubled and prone to violence and some of them might be self-identified Goths. If you know anyone who hurts or tortures animals, or even kills them, they probably need psychological help. If anyone you know talks about hurting others, they are also in need of help. And if you know of anyone who speaks about killing himself or herself, encourage that person to talk to someone about it.

Chapter Three

Gothic Lifestyle

When Goths are alone, they do a lot of the same things non-Goths do—eat, read, relax. But many Goths tend to do a lot of thinking and also a lot of creating— whether it be painting, writing poetry, or playing musical instruments. And, contrary to the stereotype, some Goths even exercise and play sports.

Although Goths may be introverted and keep to themselves, many are very social. Oftentimes they do spend their social time with other Goths because of their shared interests. But the Goth philosophy does not require that Goths only interact with each other. They are usually very open-minded and likely have a wide range of friends.

Like other people, Goths like to get together and just hang out. They spend a lot of time talking about their ideas and philosophies, exchanging their views on the world, life, death, and art. Although some watch a lot of horror movies or *Buffy the Vampire Slayer* and *The X-Files*, not all of them do.

Common Ground

Music plays an enormous role in Goth subculture, so the nightclub is an important meeting ground for the Goth who is of age. Goth clubs simply cater to and provide a welcome atmosphere for those who prescribe to the Goth philosophy. Some cities and towns have Goth clubs; in other places certain clubs have special Goth nights, where Goth music is played and Goths congregate.

Music is a strong common bond that holds the Goth social scene together. Therefore, independent music stores are a popular meeting place for many young Goths. Those in the Goth scene might also get together with each other in coffee shops, thrift stores that carry Goth wear, or in vintage clothing stores.

Another place that Goths frequent is the graveyard. Cemeteries are quiet and tranquil places, filled with sculptures and mausoleums (large stone tombs above ground). Statues of mythological figures, gargoyles, and other decorative stonework also grace the grave-yard grounds. These are great places to walk around and discover thought-provoking inscriptions and insights into life and death on tombstones. Some

Goths are often drawn to the tranquility of cemeteries.

Goths find the mystery of the cemetery fascinating and inspiring, and a great place to draw, paint, relax, or write.

Goth culture also has a tremendous presence on the Internet. Goths who participate in Internet activities call themselves Cybergoths. Many of them put their creative talents to good use by designing their own Web sites. Some post their poetry or their lyrics. Others feature their photographs or artwork. Goths can join newsgroups or surf the Web and discover many Goth-oriented sites. There are listings of clubs worldwide, lists of Goth and industrial music, histories of the Goth scene, tips and pointers for Goths, and recommendations for Goth fashion. Some Web zines—

alternative Web-based magazines—offer some good classic and contemporary horror stories.

Sexuality

Goths are very open-minded, imaginative, and highly sensuous people. They tend to be more willing to explore and experiment with many different ways of life, especially where gender identity and sexuality is concerned. Goth fashion and style often reflect a blurring of traditional female and male roles. Goth men and boys sometimes wear lipstick, nail polish, and other makeup. Many do this simply for dramatic effect and to create a more striking appearance. Some Goth men and boys wear women's clothing. They often do this to experiment with their identity. Others might do it simply to shock people. The same goes for girls and women who wear men's clothing. Although they may experiment with these different gender roles, it is not necessarily a reflection of their sexual interests or gender identity.

Religion

The Goth scene is very tolerant of many different types of religion. Therefore, people who hold atypical beliefs or practice unconventional (uncommon) religions might be drawn to the Goth culture. Some are Christians, while others practice new-age spirituality,

Goths are often drawn to religious symbols, like the Celtic cross.

shamanism (a religion in which a priest—a shaman—sees spirits, gods, and demons and practices magic), or paganism. Some Goths are very religious, others merely dabble in faith, and still others are atheists (believe in no god). However, since many Goths are intensely interested in things that are mysterious, they are often attracted to religious imagery, songs with religious themes, and religious jewelry and artifacts (crucifixes, Celtic crosses, ancient Egyptian ankhs, pentagrams). Sometimes Goths wear the religious jewelry for superficial spiritual reasons (they might like the idea of what the jewelry represents, but do not follow the religion), while others may wear the jewelry just to be fashionable.

Wicca is a contemporary version of a pagan religion, based on living in harmony with nature.

Paganism

Paganism has been around for thousands of years. It is an ancient religion in which more than one god is worshiped—people worship several different gods, goddesses, and different aspects of nature. There are many different types of paganism, but the one most commonly recognized by the general public is Wicca or Witchcraft. Pagans often draw from many different types of religion—such as Wicca, different mythologies, druidism, and shamanism—to create a version of spiritual beliefs that works for them.

Wicca is a contemporary version of a pagan religion dating from pre-Christian times, and it is one of the fastest-growing religions in the United States. Like the ancient spiritual roots from which it came, Wicca is based on living in harmony with nature and Earth's creatures. Wiccans worship different gods and goddesses, and celebrate ancient sacred rites during winter and summer solstices and equinoxes. Wicca is also referred to as witchcraft, and most Wiccans call themselves witches. They tend to worship alone or with small groups, although for some special occasions they meet in much larger groups.

Witchcraft combines science, philosophy, and art to generate a psychic energy to create magic. There are many different types of witches, and most witches don't use magic to harm or curse anyone. They view themselves as benevolent (good, not evil) figures who are in tune with nature and the forces around them.

Many Wiccans are mistakenly associated with satanism, which is an entirely different faith.

Satanism

Although satanists represent a very, very small part of the Goth scene, there are some Goths that practice the satanist faith. But contrary to what many people believe, most satanists do not worship the devil.

There are two different types of satanists. Traditional satanists believe in the being Satan, and worship it as their leader. Modern satanists, who follow the ideas of Anton LeVay (who wrote *The Satanic Bible* and created modern satanism about thirty years ago), believe that Satan is just an idea and not an actual being. They do not believe in God or the devil; they don't believe in any god. Although the religion itself is not "evil," satanists do advocate revenge. The main ideas of the satanist faith are that people should be responsible for their own actions and that magic exists.

Christian Goths

Although Christianity may seem to go against the Gothic philosophy, some Goths are Christian Goths or Born-Again Christian Goths. As discussed in an article in *Christian Century* about the Christian Goth movement, "the Goth outlook is aligned with the Christian perspective in many ways—like Christianity, Goth culture acknowledges human fallenness and suffering." Goths are very consciously aware of life and death, so Christian Goths argue that there is no contradiction or conflict in being a Christian and a Goth. Many Christians (and others) mistakenly believe that the Goth interest in darkness is an interest in evil. This is untrue—most Goths want to understand darkness and death so that they may truly experience life.

Vampirism

Many non-Goths mistakenly believe that Goths are vampires or want to become vampires. This is another misconception. Since many Goths love horror stories and movies, naturally they are interested in Dracula and other vampires. They find the myth and the legend intriguing. They have an interest in the idea but not the reality. Other Goths think the whole idea of vampirism is ridiculous. Even if Goths dress like the vampires with fangs and a black cape that we've seen in the movies or read about in books, they are probably doing so to create an air of mystery, or to revel in the symbolism of vampires—fearlessness, sensuality, freedom, power, and most of all, immortality. Others dress like vampires simply to shock people or because they like the way it looks.

Battling Stereotypes

As we've said again and again in this book, there is no one type of Goth. Although most Goths are nonviolent, the media and the actions of a few fringe characters have led many people to mistakenly believe that all Goths are vampires, killers, racists, or gun-wielding maniacs. Every Goth, and every person, is an individual with his or her own feelings and opinions. How would you feel if someone judged you based only on the way you look? You are much more than the way you dress; you have your own thoughts, personality, and ideas.

Someone who dresses all in black isn't necessarily a vampire; and a girl who listens to Marilyn Manson is probably not a Satan worshipper.

Talking to others, listening to their thoughts, trying to find things in common with them, and learning from your differences can be a rewarding way to interact with people. Maybe you'll even realize through such interactions that Goths are actually courageous for going against the mainstream.

Chapter Four

Gothic Fashion

Fashion plays an enormous role in Gothic culture. Many Goths use fashion, makeup, and hairstyles as ways of expressing themselves. Although there are different ways to dress Goth, there are some common styles that Goths gravitate toward. And while it's true that many Goths take great care about their appearance, dressing Goth does not necessarily make a person Goth. There are some Goths that live and think Goth, yet they don't wear clothing typical of most Goths. Gothic fashion also varies from place to place. Goths in Germany might dress differently from Goths in San Francisco. Spanish Goths have different hairstyles than their peers in Scotland. Some Goth clubs attract a more romantic Gothic style, while other clubs lure a more rebellious and tougher-looking Goth.

The majority of Goths dress in a style that is quite different from the mainstream. This tends to make Goths very recognizable by other Goths and to the public in general. And although many Goths share a similar aesthetic, dressing Goth is about using your imagination and finding your own personal style.

As we mentioned earlier, in the Goth community it's not uncommon to see boys and men wearing nail polish, skirts, and other types of women's clothing. Some simply do this because they like to play around with traditional ideas of what it means to be male, to experiment with their gender identity. Others simply like women's fashion. Other boys might be doing it simply for shock value. Similarly, women often wear men's clothing for a variety of reasons. They may be exploring a more masculine role or may just feel more comfortable in those clothes. In general, Goths tend to be very open to exploring gender identity and playing with conventional rules of what it means to be male or female.

Some of the more elaborate and fancy Goth clothing can get very expensive, so the best places to shop are often thrift or vintage stores. These stores are easier to find in cities, but even most small towns have a Salvation Army, Goodwill, or other such stores or used clothing outlets.

Popular Goth Clothing

- Black or dark-colored velvet skirts, dresses, and vests
- Doc Martens or combat boots
- White poet's shirts
- Rubber, leather, or vinyl gear
- Corsets
- Pagan or Christian jewelry
- Buckles, pointy shoes, and ripped fishnets

Black

Without a doubt, black is the most popular color for Goths, and it's no surprise. There's no other color that so clearly represents the darkness that so many Goths think about and explore. Although it's unclear as to why the first contemporary Goths started to wear black, the trend may have begun as a reaction against the glitzy and flashy clothes of the early 1970s. The first Goth bands, such as Bauhaus and Siouxsie and the Banshees, set the standard for black in Gothic fashion.

Black is a very striking and dramatic color. When worn with pale face makeup, it creates a theatrical look by drawing attention to the skin. Any clothing that is black might be considered Goth, from T-shirts and jeans, to leggings and tights, to elaborate capes, long skirts, corsets, and chokers.

Besides black, Goths also wear other dark colors such as deep (blood) reds, and hunter greens. White is probably the second most popular Goth color because of the striking contrast it provides to black and other dark colors.

Romantic and Victorian Wear

Many Goths are lovers of Romantic literature and poetry. They find the freedom, sensuality, passion, and intense emotionalism of the movement inspiring. So it's not surprising that the fashion of that time—poet's shirts, long and flowing skirts and dresses—are worn by certain segments of the Gothic community. These styles make the wearers feel free and sensuous, and they usually reflect a certain artistic sensibility. Other Gothic fashion is influenced by the Victorian period. Women and men don velvet vests, opera capes, and white ruffled shirts—typical of the Victorian era. The white ruffled shirt is also popular because it is part of the vampire "uniform" we've seen in *Dracula, Interview with the Vampire*, and other vampire films.

Makeup

Elaborate and dramatic makeup is popular for both males and females in the Goth scene. One of the most

White ruffled shirts, like this one sported by Tom Cruise in *Interview with the Vampire,* are a popular element of Goth fashion.

common looks is pale skin—achieved by wearing pale foundation or powder—contrasted with dark eyeshadow, and heavily applied black eyeliner. The resulting appearance, which is further enhanced by dark hair and clothing, is theatrical, and often makes people resemble the living dead.

Wearing dark lipstick is also very common among Goths. Black, blood red, and bluish, or purplish shades are all very popular colors. And for a final touch, Goths often pluck their eyebrows until they are almost completely gone, and then draw them in with dark eyebrow pencil.

Many contemporary Goths, both girls and boys, also wear nail polish. There are many different colors available now that are especially appealing to the Goth sensibility—sparkly blues, deep purples, crimson reds, and, of course, black.

Hair

Many Goths experiment with different hairstyles. Some use extensions. Others use a lot of hairspray to make their hair stand straight up. Others work to achieve a tangled, chaotic look. Some have long, flowing gorgeous hair. Others wear the punk-influenced mohawk style or the white-blond Billy Idol look. A style popular among Goths in the United Kingdom is crimped hair. As with the many other things they do, Goths' hairstyles reflect their diversity and originality. Many Goths dye their hair. The most common color is black, but red, burgundy, blue, magenta, yellow, and white are also popular colors.

Jewelry and Other Accessories

Some Goths wear a great deal of jewelry, and it's almost always silver. Goths usually don't wear gold, but some might wear copper. Many Goths decorate themselves with religious symbols, although most of them do it only for fashion. They are drawn to the mysticism, power, and mystery of the symbols. The pentagram (a pagan symbol) is very popular, as are ancient Egyptian symbols (such as the ankh, the

Ornate silver rings and necklaces are common accessories among Goths.

horu, and the Eye of Ra). Many Goths wear crucifixes or Celtic crosses. Some wear skulls, coffins, and other horror-oriented items as jewelry.

Chains (hanging from clothing or around the neck as a necklace) are also common, as are spiked or studded bracelets or rings. Male and female Goths also might wear chokers or collars. Some male and female Goths are spotted wearing long satin gloves.

Chapter Five | Gothic Music, Literature, and Film

As we have mentioned, the arts, including music, literature, and film, have played a key role in the development of Goth culture.

Music

Many people believe that music started the contemporary Goth subculture. While there are some Goths who claim that the subculture came together before people began labeling this music Goth, almost all Goths agree that the music provides the base for the Goth scene.

As you now know, Goth bands were an offshoot of the punk scene of the 1970s. Bands such as Bauhaus, Siouxsie and the Banshees, Joy Division, and The Cure had a punk sound, but their songs had a very dark feel to them. The music was often eerie and moody, and the lyrics were melancholy, serious, and dark.

Much Goth music is richly textured, orchestral, or has multiple layers of guitar with special effects to make it sound distorted or otherworldly. It might feature such instruments as the harpsichord, the violin, the cello, organs, pipes, or synthesized versions of those instruments. It often sounds like it's coming from a cathedral or a haunted house. Not surprisingly, Goth lyrics often revolve around doom and death. The tone is serious and gloomy. But Goth lyrics are also often mystical, mentioning vampires, dungeons, castles, or spiritual images.

Other Goth bands, such as Dead Can Dance and the Cocteau Twins, have a much dreamier sound, with ethereal effects and high female voices. These bands are less punk than the ones previously mentioned and more experimental and technologically progressive. Such bands as Sisters of Mercy are more rock oriented. Another type of Goth music is very similar to heavy metal. Goth metal (or Death Metal) is influenced by such bands as Black Sabbath and includes Type O Negative.

Since the early scene, Goth music has gone through different phases and changes. Some bands have separated, or changed their musical direction, moving entirely away from Goth. Others still play some Goth but also play different kinds of music. Many Goths also listen to industrial music (music influenced by techno and electronica), such as Marilyn Manson and Nine Inch Nails.

The music of bands like The Cure is a key element of the Goth subculture.

Popular Goth Bands

Alien Sex Fiend

All About Eve

Bauhaus

The Birthday Party

Black Tape for a Blue Girl

Nick Cave

Christian Death

Cocteau Twins

The Cranes

The Cure

Dead Can Dance

Death in June

Echo and the Bunnymen

Faith and the Muse

Fields of Nephilim

Joy Division

London After Midnight

Love Is Colder Than Death

The Mission

Rosetta Stone

Nick Cave's music and lyrics deal with some of the same dark themes explored by Gothic writers like Flannery O'Connor.

Sex Gang Children

Siouxsie and the Banshees

Sisters of Mercy

Southern Death Cult (later, Death Cult, and finally just The Cult)

Suspiria

Switchblade Symphony

Type O Negative

Literature

Because Goths tend to be creative, imaginative, and soulful people, many of them love to read good stories, poetry, and novels. Many Goths love fairy tales or fantasy stories. The occult and the supernatural often enchant Goths. So a good read to a Goth could mean a scary horror story by Edgar Allan Poe, a dark and romantic poem by Lord Byron, a mystical novel by Storm Constantine, or an Anne Rice vampire story.

Classical Gothic novels of the nineteenth century are also very popular with today's Goths. Some examples of Goth favorites from this era include Bram Stoker's *Dracula* and Mary Wollstonecraft Shelley's *Frankenstein*. Gothic novels usually take place in desolate, remote settings, and feature turreted castles, ghosts, horrific and macabre imagery, thunderstorms, and lots of misery and drama. Goths also love poetry that explores such themes as the supernatural, and tortured love.

Nowadays, Goths have many contemporary Goth writers to choose from, ranging from Goth hero Anne Rice to cult favorite Poppy Z. Brite. Many Goths also enjoy science fiction.

Popular Goth Writers

Dante Alighieri—Italian poet; wrote *The Inferno*

Charles Baudelaire—sensuous French symbolist poet, influenced by Edgar Allan Poe

Ray Bradbury—a science fiction favorite; works include *Something Wicked This Way Comes*

Poppy Z. Brite—works include *Lost Souls*

Anthony Burgess—British author of *A Clockwork Orange*

Lord Byron (George Gordon Byron)—a classic melancholy, brooding, romantic poet

Albert Camus—works include *The Stranger*

Storm Constantine—writes about the occult and some ancient mythological themes

Fyodor Dostoyevsky—Russian novelist; works include *Notes From the Underground*

Edgar Allan Poe's tales of the supernatural are popular reading among Goths.

William Gibson—a favorite of Cybergoths; science fiction works include *Neuromancer*

Stephen King—modern-day horror novelist; works include *Salem's Lot* and *The Shining*

H. P. Lovecraft—writer of horror tales; wrote the favorite Gothic short story "The Call of Cthulhu"

John Milton—English poet; works include the 1667 masterpiece *Paradise Lost*

Frederich Nietzche—German philosopher who wrote *Beyond Good and Evil*

Joyce Carol Oates—contemporary American author who explores Gothic themes

Edgar Allan Poe—a Goth hero; classic writer of poems and short stories of horror; works include "The Pit and the Pendulum" and "Murders in the Rue Morgue"

Ann Radcliffe—English writer who authored the classic Gothic novel, *The Mysteries of Udolpho*

Anne Rice—American novelist; works include the Vampire Chronicles *(Interview with the Vampire, The Vampire Lestat, Queen of the Damned, The Tale of the Body Thief);* also *The Witching Hour* and *The Mummy*

Jean-Paul Sartre—French philosopher, dramatist, and poet whose works include *Being and Nothingness*

Mary Wollstonecraft Shelley—English novelist; wrote the 1818 classic *Frankenstein*

Percy Bysshe Shelley—English romantic poet; his work explored good and evil, and the supernatural

Bram Stoker—wrote the classic *Dracula* in 1897

Leo Tolstoy—Russian novelist; works include *War and Peace*

Movies

Goths love a good classic horror flick, vampire films, and science fiction. As is usually true with all other types of art that Goths love, Goths enjoy films that are experimental, imaginative, and original. Goths like some mainstream movies with Gothic themes, and some more offbeat, cult classics.

Popular Goth Movies

Beetlejuice—A contemporary, strange, and highly original dark comedy directed by Tim Burton

The Cabinet of Dr. Caligari—A classic silent horror film from 1920; an example of German expressionism

Tim Burton has directed several films with a Goth sensibility, including *Edward Scissorhands* starring Johnny Depp.

A Clockwork Orange—A science fiction horror based on the novel by Anthony Burgess and directed by the late Stanley Kubrick

The Craft—A contemporary film that features witchcraft and a Goth-type lead character played by Fairuza Balk

Cronos—A Mexican horror fantasy about vampires

The Crow—A contemporary cult Goth classic about a murdered man who comes back to life looking for revenge; Brandon Lee, the lead, died during the filming

Dracula—The classic 1931 tale of our favorite vampire played by Bela Lugosi; film remade in 1992 by Francis Ford Coppola

Edward Scissorhands—Another Tim Burton film, it centers around a Goth-type figure with scissors for hands who lives in suburbia

Gothic—A 1987 movie based on the 1816 night when a meeting between Lord Byron, Percy Bysshe Shelley, and Mary Wollstonecraft Shelley inspired Mary to write *Frankenstein*

Heathers—A contemporary, dark humor classic starring Winona Ryder and Christian Slater

The Hunger—A Goth favorite filmed in 1983, with appearances by Bauhaus's Peter Murphy,

David Bowie, and sexy vampires, plus great horror imagery

The Lost Boys—A 1987 film about young California vampires

Nosferatu—The unforgettable 1922 classic tale of the living dead; see also the 1979 remake

The Rocky Horror Picture Show—A cult musical film that has become an event when shown in theaters; people throw rice, and mime the action; with Susan Sarandon, Tim Curry, and the "Time Warp" song

Rowing the Wind—Another movie based on the eerie nightmarish evening that inspired Mary Wollstonecraft Shelley to write *Frankenstein*

Glossary

aesthetic   A particular idea or concept of beauty.

barbarian   Lacking culture or civility; savage.

equinox   The two times each year (March 21 and September 21) when the sun crosses the equator and the hours of day and night are of equal length.

grotesque   Bizarre; very different from what is typical or expected; based on fantasy.

macabre   Related to death.

mainstream   Popular and common thought and activity.

medieval   Relating to the period of the Middle Ages, from the fifth to the fifteenth centuries.

melancholy   Feeling thoughtful; also sad, depressed, or dismal.

pacifists   People who don't believe in the use of violence or war to settle problems.

paganism   A religion in which people worship nature and more than one god.

prejudice   Judging someone based on a preconceived notion.

Renaissance   A period from the fourteenth to the seventeenth centuries, that was marked by great discoveries in science and the arts.

Romantic   Relating to the literary and philosophical movement that began in the eighteenth century, in which imagination, the emotions, and nature were emphasized.

scapegoats   People that are blamed for the actions of others.

sensibility   Awareness of sensations or emotions; the ability to experience, or extreme sensitivity to sensations or emotions.

shamanism   A faith, common among Native Americans, in which a medicine man or witch with magical powers communicates with spirits.

solstice   The two times each year (June 22 and December 22) when the earth is at its closest or farthest from the sun.

stereotypes   Characteristics attached to a group, culture, or race; usually oversimplified and often negative and misleading.

supernatural   Having to do with spirits, ghosts, and other entities that are unseen.

unconventional   Uncommon; not typical or ordinary.

For More Information

Web Sites

Academia Gothic
A Web site created by the Ice Princess, it is filled with insights into the Goth scene.
http://wwwblarg.net/~icprncs

Author, Anne Rice's official Web site
http://www.annerice.com

Bauhaus's official Web site
http://www.bauhausmusik.com

Dark Side of the Net
This Web site has many links to other Goth Web sites from all over the world
http://www.darklinks.com

The Gothic Literature page
http://members.aol.com/iamudolpho/basic.html

A History of Goth
This site traces the origins of the modern Goth scene
and gives an outline of what being Goth means today.
http://www.scathe.demon.co.uk/intro.htm

Sisters of Mercy's official Web site
http://www.thesistersofmercy.com

For Further Reading

Fiction

Bradbury, Ray. *Something Wicked This Way Comes*. New York: Avon Books, 1998.

Burgess, Anthony. *A Clockwork Orange*. Cutchgue, NY: Buccaneer Books, Inc., 1996.

Gibson, William. *Neuromancer*. New York: Ace Books, 1986.

King, Stephen. *Salem's Lot*. New York: Doubleday, 1975.

———. *The Shining*. New York: Doubleday, 1990.

Radcliffe, Ann. *The Mysteries of Udolpho*. New York: Oxford University Press, Inc., 1998.

Rice, Anne. *Interview with the Vampire*. New York: Ballentine Books, Inc., 1986.

Shelley, Mary Wollstonecraft. *Frankenstein*. New York: Random House, Inc., 1999.

Index

Index

About the Author

Kerry Acker is a freelance editor and writer based in Brooklyn, New York.

Photo Credits

Cover and pp. 2 and 43 by Heather Halliday; p. 32 Adriana Skura; p. 29 © Super Stock; p. 11 © North Wind Picture Archives; pp. 13 and 31 © Archive Photos; pp. 17, 22, 26, 41, 46, 48, and 54 © The Everett Collection; p. 51 © Bettmann/Corbis.

Acknowledgments

Special thanks to Jim, Sarah, Michelle, and to Erica Smith at the Rosen Publishing Group.